Interview Questions & A

NGULARJS

100+ Frequently asked Interview Q & A

90% Frequently asked Interview
Q & A in Angular JS

By Bandana Ojha

Introduction

The authors of this book "Interview Questions & Answers in Angular JS" conducted so many interviews at various companies and meticulously collected the most effective questions with simple, straightforward explanations. Rather than going through comprehensive, textbook-sized reference guides, this book includes only the information required to start his/her career as an Angular JS developer. Answers of all the questions are short and to the point. We assure that you will get 90% frequently asked interview questions and answers going through this book.

Good luck to ALL !!!

1. What is AngularJS?

AngularJS is an open source JavaScript framework that helps to create dynamic Web applications. It supports to use HTML as the template language and enables the developer to create extended HTML tags that help to represent the application's components more clearly. These tags make the code efficient by reducing the lines of code that a developer may need to write when using JavaScript.

2. What are Angular Expressions?

In AngularJS, expressions are used to bind application data to HTML. AngularJS resolves the expression and return the result exactly where the expression is written.

Expressions are written inside double braces {{expression}}.They can also be written inside a directive: ng-bind="expression".

3.What is key difference between angular expressions and JavaScript expressions?

Difference between AngularJS Expressions and JavaScript expressions are:

AngularJS expressions can be written inside HTML, while JavaScript expressions cannot.

AngularJS expressions support filters, while JavaScript expressions do not.

AngularJS expressions do not support conditionals, loops, and exceptions, while JavaScript expressions do.

4. What are the advantages of AngularJS?

Following are the advantages of AngularJS.

AngularJS provides capability to create Single Page Application in a very clean and maintainable way.

With AngularJS, developer writes less code and gets more functionality.

AngularJS supports powerful data binding; it is two-way data binding with the help of HTML & scope.

AngularJS has good support over the internet and over time it has new changes available for developers. It also supports IE, Opera, Safari, and Chrome.

In AngularJS, views are pure html pages, and controllers written in JavaScript do the business processing.

AngularJS has easily testable Unit testing, it doesn't need to load all the app, just loading that specific module is enough to start unit testing.

5. What are the disadvantages of AngularJS?

Following are the disadvantages of AngularJS.

Not Secure – Being JavaScript only framework, application written in AngularJS are not safe. Server-side authentication and authorization is must to keep an application secure.

Not degradable – If your application user disables JavaScript then user will just see the basic page and nothing more.

6. What is data binding in AngularJs?

Data binding is the connection bridge between view and business logic (view model) of the application. Data binding in AngularJs is the automatic synchronization between the model and view. When the model changes, the view is automatically updated and vice versa. AngularJs support one-way binding as well as two-way binding.

7. What is scope in AngularJS?

Scope refers to the application model, it acts like glue between application controller and the view. Scopes are arranged in hierarchical structure and impersonate the DOM (Document Object Model) structure of the application. It can watch expressions and propagate events.

8.What are the characteristics of "scope"?

Following are the characteristics of scope:

-To observer model mutations scopes provide APIs ($watch).

T-o propagate any model changes through the system into the view from outside of the Angular realm.

-A scope inherits properties from its parent scope, while providing access to shared model properties, scopes can be nested to isolate application components.

-Scope provides context against which expressions are evaluated.

9. What is $scope and $rootScope?

$scope - A $scope is a JavaScript object which is used for communication between controller and view. Basically, $scope binds a view (DOM element) to the model and functions defined in a controller.

$rootScope - The $rootScope is the top-most scope. An app can have only one $rootScope which will be shared among all the components of an app. Hence it acts like a global variable. All other $scopes are children of the $rootScope.

10. What is scope inheritance?

Ans. The $scope object used by views in AngularJS are organized into a hierarchy. There is a root scope, and the $rootScope can has one or more child scopes. Each controller has its own $scope (which is a child of the $rootScope), so whatever variables you create on $scope within controller, these variables are accessible by the view based on this controller.

11. What is DI (Dependency Injection)?

DI or Dependency Injection is a software design pattern that deals with how code gets hold of its dependencies. In order to retrieve elements of the application which is required to be configured when module gets loaded , the operation "config" uses dependency injection.

12. How an object or function can get a hold of its dependencies ?

These are the ways that object uses to hold of its dependencies

-Typically using the new operator, dependency can be created

-By referring to a global variable, dependency can be looked up

-Dependency can be passed into where it is required

13. What are directives in AngularJS?

AngularJS extends the behavior of HTML and DOM elements with new attributes called Directives. It directs the AngularJS's HTML compiler ($compile) to attach a unique action to that DOM element. This AngularJS component starts with the prefix "ng."

14.Name some commonly used directives in Angular JS application ?

Following is the list of AngularJS built-in directives.

ng-bind – The ng-bind directive tells AngularJS to replace the content of an HTML element with the value of a given variable, or expression.

If there is any change in the value of the given variable or expression, then the content of the specified HTML element will also be updated accordingly. It supports one-way binding only.

ng-model – This directive is used to bind the value of HTML controls (input, select, text area) to application data. It is responsible for linking the view into the model.

Directives such as 'input', 'text area', and 'select' require it. It supports two-way data binding.

ng-class – This directive dynamically binds one or more CSS classes to an HTML element. The value of the ng-class directive can be a string, an object, or an array.

ng-app – Just like the "Main()" function of Java language, this directive marks the beginning of the application to AngularJS's HTML compiler ($compile). If we do not use this directive first, an error gets generated.

ng-init – This is used to initialize the application data so that we can use it in the block where it is declared. If an application requires local data like a single value or an array of values, this can be achieved using the ng-init directive.

ng-repeat – This repeats a set of HTML statements for the defined number of times. The set of HTML statements will be repeated once per item in a collection. This collection must be an array or an object.

15. What are the attributes can be used during creation of a new AngularJS Directives?

The following attributes can be used during creation of a new AngularJS Directives,

Restrict

The restrict attribute is how AngularJS triggers the directive inside a template. The default value of the restrict option is "A". The value of "A" causes the directives to be triggered on the attribute name. Other than "A", restrict option has "E" (only match element name), "C" (only match class name) and "M" (only match the comment name) or any combination among four options.

TemplateUrl

The templateUrl attribute tells the AngularJS HTML compiler to replace custom directive inside a template with HTML content located inside a separate file. The link-Menu (say, our custom directive name) attribute will be replaced with the content of our original menu template file.

Template

Specify an inline template as a string. Not used if you're specifying your template as a URL.

Replace

If true, replace the current element. If false or unspecified, append this directive to the current element.

Transclude

Let's you move the original children of a directive to a location inside the new template.

Scope

Create a new scope for this directive rather than inheriting the parent scope.

Controller

Create a controller which publishes an API for communicating across directives.

Require

Require that another directive be present for this directive to function correctly.

Link

Programmatically modify resulting DOM element instances, add event listeners, and set up data binding.

Compile

Programmatically modify the DOM template for features across copies of a directive, as when used in other directives. Your compile function can also return link functions to modify the resulting element instances.

16. Which are the three core directives of AngularJS?

Following are the three core directives of AngularJS.

ng-app – This directive defines and links an AngularJS application to HTML.

ng-model – This directive binds the values of AngularJS application data to HTML input controls.

ng-bind – This directive binds the AngularJS Application data to HTML tags.

17. What is Model in AngularJS?

Ans. Models are plain old JavaScript objects that represent data used by your app. Models are also used to represent your app's current state.

18. What is ViewModel in AngularJS?

A viewmodel is an object that provides specific data and methods to maintain specific views. Basically, it is a $scope object which lives within your AngularJS app's controller. A viewmodel is associated with a HTML element with the ng-model and ng-bind directives.

19. What is MVC?

Model View Controller or MVC as it is popularly called, is a software design pattern for developing web applications. A Model View Controller pattern is made up of the following three parts:

Model – It is the lowest level of the pattern responsible for maintaining data.

View – It is responsible for displaying all or a portion of the data to the user.

Controller – It is a software Code that controls the interactions between the Model and View.

20. Is AngularJS extensible?

Yes, In AngularJS we can create custom directive to extend AngularJS existing functionalities.

Custom directives are used in AngularJS to extend the functionality of HTML. Custom directives are defined using "directive" function. A custom directive simply replaces the element for which it is activated. AngularJS application during bootstrap finds the matching elements and do one-time activity using its compile() method of the custom directive then process the element using link() method of the custom directive based on the scope of the directive.

21. What is Controller in AngularJS?

Controller is constructor function in Angular Controller. When a Controller is attached to the DOM with use the ng-controller, Angular will instantiate a new Controller object using constructor function

22. What are different states of a form in AngularJS?

The AngularJS form goes to the following states, starting from the form rendering and when the user has finished the filling of form.

State 1: pristine and invalid - When the form is first time rendered and the user has not interacted with the form yet.

State 2: dirty and invalid - User has interacted with the form, but form validity has not been satisfied, yet.

State 3: dirty and valid - User has finished the filling of form and the entire form validations has been satisfied

23. What is string interpolation in Angular.js ?

In Angular.js the compiler during the compilation process matches text and attributes using interpolate service to see if they contain embedded expressions. As part of normal digest cycle these expressions are updated and registered as watches.

24. What methods $resource service object support?

The $resource service object supports the following methods:

1. get()

2. query()

3. save()

4. remove()

5. delete()

25. What is difference between $window and window in AngularJS?

$window is an Angular service which reference to the browser's window object. The window object is globally available in JavaScript; it causes testability problems, because it is a global variable. Angular refer to it through the $window service, so that it can be overridden, removed or mocked for testing.

26. What is the difference between one-way binding and two-way binding ?

In One-Way data binding, view (UI part) not updates automatically when data model changed. We need to write custom code to make it updated every time.

ng-bind has one-way data binding.

While in two-way binding scope variable will change its value every time its data model changed is assigned to a different value.

27. What is the difference between a link and compile in Angular JS?

Compile function: To template DOM manipulation and to gather all the directives, the compile function is used.

Link function: To register DOM listeners as well as for the instance DOM manipulation, the Link function is used.

28.What is deep linking in AngularJS?

Deep linking allows you to encode the state of application in the URL so that it can be bookmarked. The application can then be restored from the URL to the same state.

29. What is an interceptor in Angular?

An interceptor is a middleware code in AngularJs where all the $http requests go through. It is attached with $httpProvider service and able to intercept request and response objects.

30.Why interceptor is used?

Interceptor Middleware is useful for error handling, authentication and other filters you want to apply on request and response.

ng-repeat – This directive is used to instantiate the template once per item from a collection.

Each template which is instantiated gets its own scope where the given loop variable is set to the current collection of items.

31. Explain Routing in Angular JS?

Routing is one the core feature of AngularJs Framework that is useful in building a single page web application with multiple views. In Angular ngRoute Module is used to implement Routing. ngView,$routeProvider,$route and $routeParams are different components of the ngRoute Module that helps to configure and mapping URL to views.

32. What is the difference between link and compile in Angular.js?

Compile function: It is used for template DOM Manipulation and collect all of the directives.

Link function: It is used for registering DOM listeners as well as instance DOM manipulation. It is executed once the template has been cloned.

33. What is the bootstrapping in AngularJS?

Bootstrapping in AngularJS is initializing or starting the Angular app. AngularJS supports automatic bootstrapping as well as manual.

34. How to do manual bootstrap in AngularJS ?

Sometimes we may need to manually initialize Angular app to have more control over the initialization process. We can do that by using angular.bootstrap() function within angular.element(document).ready() function. AngularJS fires this function when the DOM is ready for manipulation. The angular.bootstrap() function takes two parameters, the document, and module name injector.

35. What makes AngularJS better ?

Registering Callbacks: There is no need to register callbacks . This makes your code simple and easy to debug.

Control HTML DOM programmatically: All the application that are created using Angular never have to manipulate the DOM although it can be done if it is required

Transfer data to and from the UI: AngularJS helps to eliminate almost all of the boiler plate like validating the form, displaying validation errors, returning to an internal model and so on which occurs due to flow of marshalling data

No initialization code: You can combine multiple modules into single modules and your angular app will be automatically initialized for newly created module and other modules will act as dependent modules for newly created module.

36. What does SPA (Single page application) mean?

SPA is a concept where rather loading pages from the server by doing post backs, we create a single shell page or master page and load the webpages inside that master page.

37. How to do email and Phone no. validation in Angular JS?

Angular form validation and ng-pattern directive can be used to validate the email and phone number in Angular JS.

38. What are the styling form that ngModel adds to CSS classes ?

ngModel adds these CSS classes to allow styling of form as well as control:

1. ng- valid

2. ng-invalid

3. ng-pristine

4. ng-dirty

39. What is the use of systemjs?

Systemjs is a client-side module bundler in angular as it loads modules (components and other files) on demand instead of loading an entire application at startup.

This largely reduces load times while starting up the app.

40.How is webpack better to use in Angular than systemjs ?

The up side of webpack over systemjs is that it bundles and creates a single file called bundle.js, which contains HTML, CSS and JS etc.

While the initial load time might take a few seconds once the app is cached it becomes lightning fast and will lead to a large boost in performance.

41. What are different ways to invoke a directive ?

There are four different ways to invoke a directive in an angular application. They are as follows.

1) As an attribute

2) As a class

3) As an element

4) As a comment

42. What is transclusion in Angular JS?

Transclusion is a very powerful and useful feature of AngularJS directives. It allows a directive to use a template while still having the ability to clone the original content and add it to the DOM. Transclusion allows directives to generate dynamic, data-driven DOM structures that create a compelling user experience.

43. What is injector?

An injector is a service locator. It is used to retrieve object instances as defined by provider, instantiate types, invoke methods and load modules. There is a single injector per Angular application, it helps to look up an object instance by its name.

44. What is linking function ?

Link combines the directives with a scope and produce a live view. For registering DOM listeners as well as updating the DOM, link function is responsible. After the template is cloned it is executed.

45. What are type of linking function?

Pre-linking function: Pre-linking function is executed before the child elements are linked. It is not considered as the safe way for DOM transformation.

Post linking function: Post linking function is executed after the child elements are linked. It is safe to do DOM transformation by post-linking function.

46. Does angular use the jQuery library?

Yes, Angular can use jQuery if it's presents in your app when the application is being bootstrapped. If jQuery is not present in your script path, Angular falls back to its own implementation of the subset of jQuery that we call jQLite.

47. What is internationalization?

Internationalization is a way to show locale specific information on a website. For example, display content of a website in English language in United States and in Danish in France.

48. How to implement internationalization in AngularJS?

AngularJS supports inbuilt internationalization for three types of filters currency, date and numbers. We only need to incorporate corresponding js according to locale of the country. By default, it handles the locale of the browser.

49. Explain Directive scopes?

There are three types of directive scopes available in Angular.

Parent Scope: is default scope

Child Scope: If the properties and functions you set on the scope are not relevant to other directives and the parent, you should probably create a new child scope.

Isolated Scope: Isolated Scope is used if the directive you are going to build is self-contained and reusable. Does not inherit from parent scope, used for private/internal use.

50. How to access parent scope from child controller in Angular JS?

In angular there is a scope variable called $parent (i.e. $scope.$parent). $parent is used to access parent scope from child controller in Angular JS.

51. What is $watch ?

When you create a data binding from somewhere in your view to a variable on the $scope object, AngularJS creates a "watch" internally. A watch means AngularJS watches changes in the variable on the $scope object. The framework is "watching" the variable. Watches are created using the $scope.$watch() function.

52. How to validate data in AngularJS?

AngularJS enriches form filling and validation. We can use $dirty and $invalid flags to do the validations in seamless way. Use no validate with a form declaration to disable any browser specific validation.

Following can be used to track error.

$dirty – states that value has been changed.

$invalid – states that value entered is invalid.

$error – states the exact error.

53. What is event handling in AngularJS?

When we want to create advanced AngularJS applications such as User Interaction Forms, then we need to handle DOM events like mouse clicks, moves, keyboard presses, change events and so on. AngularJS has a simple model for how to add event listeners. We can attach an event listener to an HTML element using one of the following AngularJS event listener directives.

54. What are typings in Angular ?

Typings is the simple way to manage and install TypeScript definitions. Typings allows the TypeScript compiler to use existing classes, properties, and so on. We can also install typings from a repository using the typings command.

55. What's the difference between statically and dynamically typed languages?

Static Typing:-

Static typing requires that all variables and function return values be typed and TypeScript is an examples of statically typed languages.

Dynamically Typing :-

Dynamically typing does not require explicit type declaration. Python and JavaScript are best examples of dynamically typed languages.

56. What is SPA (Single page application) in AngularJS?

Single-Page Applications (SPAs) are web applications that load a single HTML page and dynamically update that page as the user interacts with the app. SPAs use AJAX and

HTML to create fluid and responsive web apps, without constant page reloads.

57. What is the difference between $watch and $observe?

$watch is a method on the scope object which is used to watch expressions. The expression can be either strings or functions. It can be called wherever you have access to scope (a controller or a directive linking function).

$observe is a method on the attrs object which is only used to observe the value change of a DOM attribute. It is only used inside directives.

58. What is Service in AngularJS?

A service is a reusable singleton object which is used to organize and share code across your app. A service can be injected into controllers, filters, directives.

AngularJS offers several built-in services (like $http, $provide, $resource, $window, $parse) which always start with $ sign.

59. What are different ways to create service in AngularJS?

There are five ways to create a service as given below:

1. Service

2. Factory

3. Provider

4. Value

5. Constant

60. What is $q service and when to use it?

$q is a service that helps you to run functions asynchronously and use their return values when they have done processing.

$q service is said to be inspired by Chris Kowal's Q library which allow users to monitor asynchronous progress by providing a "promise" as a return from a call.

It is good when you need to process a number of asynchronous activities simultaneously. The $q.all() function lets you trigger several callbacks at the same time and use a single then function to join them all together.

61. How to manage cookie in AngularJS?

Ans. AngularJS provides ngCookies module for reading and writing browser cookies. To use it include the angular-cookies.js file and set ngCookies as a dependency in your angular app. This module provides two services for cookie management: $cookies and $cookieStore.

62. What is difference between $cookies and $cookieStore service?

$cookies - This service provides read/write access to browser's cookies.

$cookiesStore - $cookieStore is a thin wrapper around $cookies. It provides a key-value (string-object) storage that is backed by session cookies. The objects which are put or retrieved from this storage are automatically serialized or deserialized by angular to JSON and vice versa.

63. What is difference between $window and window in AngularJS?

$window is an Angular service which reference to the browser's window object. The window object is globally available in JavaScript; it causes testability problems, because it is a global variable. Angular refer to it through the $window service, so that it can be overridden, removed or mocked for testing.

64. What is service method?

Using service method, we define a service and then assign method to it. We've also injected an already available service to it.

65. What is factory method?

Using factory method, we first define a factory and then assign method to it.

66.What are the differences between service and factory methods?

factory method is used to define a factory which can later be used to create services as and when required whereas service method is used to create a service whose purpose is to do some defined task.

67. What is provider?

Provider is used by AngularJS internally to create services, factory etc. during config phase(phase during which AngularJS bootstraps itself).

68. Which components can be injected as a dependency in AngularJS?

AngularJS provides a supreme Dependency Injection mechanism. It provides following core components which can be injected into each other as dependencies.

value

factory

service

provider

constant

69. What is the difference between Kris Kowal's Q and $q?

There are two main differences between Kris Kowal's Q and $q:

1. $q is integrated with the $rootScope.Scope Scope model observation mechanism in angular, which means faster propagation of resolution or rejection into your models and avoiding unnecessary browser repaints, which would result in flickering UI.

2. Q has many more features than $q, but that comes at a cost of bytes. $q is tiny but contains all the important functionality needed for common async tasks.

70. What is AngularJS digest cycle?

AngularJS digest cycle is the process behind Angular JS data binding.

In each digest cycle, Angular compares the old and the new version of the scope model values. The digest cycle is triggered automatically. We can also use $apply() if we want to trigger the digest cycle manually.

71. What is routing in AngularJS?

It is concept of switching views. AngularJS based controller decides which view to render based on the business logic.

72. How to implement routing in AngularJS?

Routing is a core feature in AngularJS. This feature is useful in building SPA (Single Page Application) with multiple views. In SPA application, all views are different Html files and we use Routing to load different parts of the application and it's helpful to divide the application logically and make it manageable. In other words, Routing helps us to divide our application in logical views and bind them with different controllers.

73. Explain callback in Node.js ?

A callback function is called at the completion of a given task. This allows other code to be run in the meantime and prevents any blocking. Being an asynchronous platform, Node.js heavily relies on callback. All APIs of Node are written to support callbacks.

74.Explain the role of REPL in Node.js ?

As the name suggests, REPL (Read Eval print Loop) performs the tasks of – Read, Evaluate, Print and Loop. The REPL in Node.js is used to execute ad-hoc JavaScript statements. The REPL shell allows entry to JavaScript directly into a shell prompt and evaluates the results. For the purpose of testing, debugging, or experimenting, REPL is very critical.

75. What are exit codes in Node.js?

Exit codes are specific codes that are used to end a "process" (a global object used to represent a node process).

76. How to use jQuery with AngularJS?

By default, AngularJS use jQLite which is the subset of jQuery. If you want to use jQuery, then simply load the jQuery library before loading the AngularJS. By doing so, Angular will skip jQLite and will started to use jQuery library.

77. What are the ways to communicate between controllers in AngularJS?

There are various different ways to share data between controllers in an AngularJS app. The most commonly used are Scope, Service, Factory and Providers.

78. What are module loaders in Angular ?

Module loaders in Angular are used to bundle different modules that contain their dependencies along with angular components into one bundle or multiple bundles (For lazy loading) and load them in the browser.

79. How AngularJS handle the security?

AngularJS provide following built-in protection from basic security holes:

1. Prevent HTML injection attacks.

2. Prevent Cross-Site-Scripting (CSS) attacks.

3. Prevent XSRF protection for server-side communication.

Also, AngularJS is designed to be compatible with other security measures like Content Security Policy (CSP), HTTPS (SSL/TLS) and server-side authentication and authorization that greatly reduce the possible attacks.

80. Why are consistent style important and what tools can be used to assure it ?

Consistent style helps team members modify projects easily without having to get used to a new style every time. Tools that can help include Standard and ESLint.

81. Is AngularJS a library, framework, plugin or a browser extension?

AngularJS fits the definition of a framework the best, even though it's much more lightweight than a typical framework and that's why many confuse it with a library. AngularJS is 100% JavaScript, 100% client side and compatible with both desktop and mobile browsers. So, it's definitely not a plugin or some other native browser extension.

82. Explain the concept of scope hierarchy? How many scope can an application have?

Each angular application consists of one root scope but may have several child scopes. As child controllers and some directives create new child scopes, application can have multiple scopes. When new scopes are formed or created they are added as a child of their parent scope. Similar to DOM, they also create a hierarchical structure.

83. What is use of $routeProvider in AngularJS ?

$routeProvider is the key service which set the configuration of urls, maps them with the corresponding html page or ng-template, and attaches a controller with the same.

84. What is constant ?

Constants are used to pass values at config phase considering the fact that value cannot be used to be passed during config phase.

mainApp.constant("configParam", "constant value");

85. Explain what is the difference between link and compile in angular.js?

Link function: It is used for registering DOM listeners as well as instance DOM manipulation. It is executed once the template has been cloned.

Compile function: It is used for template DOM Manipulation and collect all of the directives.

86. What is Restangular?

Restangular is an Angular service specifically designed simply to fetch data from the rest of the world. To use

Restangular you need to link the restangular.js file and include Restangular resource as a dependency within your angular app.

87. Explain the role of $routeProvider in AngularJS?

The $routeProvider is used to configure roots within an AngularJS application. It can be used to link a URL with a corresponding HTML page or template, and a controller (if applicable).

88. What are the filters in AngularJS?

Filters select a subset of items from an array and return a new array. Filters are used to show filtered items from a list of items based on defined criteria.

89. How lowercase filter works?

Lowercase filter converts a text to lower case text.

In below example, we've added lowercase filter to an expression using pipe character. Here we've added lowercase filter to print employee name in all lowercase letters.

Enter first name:<input type = "text" ng-model = "employee.firstName">

Enter last name: <input type = "text" ng-model = " employee.lastName">

Name in Upper Case: {{ employee.fullName() | lowercase}}

90.What is currency filter?

Currency filter formats text in a currency format.

In below example, we've added currency filter to an expression returning number using pipe character. Here we've added currency filter to print salary using currency format.

Enter salary: <input type = "text" ng-model = " employee.salary">

salary: {{ employee.salary | currency}}

91. How to make an ajax call using Angular JS?

AngularJS provides $https: control which works as a service to make ajax call to read data from the server. The server makes a database call to get the desired records. AngularJS needs data in JSON format. Once the data is ready, $https: can be used to get the data from server.

92. What is Angular Prefixes $ and $$?

To prevent accidental name collisions with your code, Angular prefixes names of public objects with $ and names of private objects with $$.

93. How to securely parse and manipulate your HTML data in AngularJS?

AngularJS provides ngSanitize module to securely parse and manipulate HTML data in your application. To use it include the angular-sanitize.js file and set ngSanitize as a dependency in your angular app.

94. What is AtScript?

AtScript is Google's new superset for JavaScript. It enhances JavaScript with new features to make it more robust. The aim of AtScript is to make type annotation data available at runtime to enhance JavaScript with type, field and metadata annotations.

95. What is AngularUI router and how it is different from ngRoute?

The UI-Router is a routing framework for AngularJS built by the AngularUI team. Unlike ngRoute, it changes your angular app views based on state of the app and not based on the route URL (ngRoute).

The UI-router helps you to create nested views, use multiple views on the same page, have multiple views that control a single view, and more.

To use it you need to include reference of ui-router.js file into your angular app.

96. Who created Angular JS ?

Initially it was developed by Misko Hevery and Adam Abrons.Currently it is being developed and maintained by Google.

97.What are ng-repeat special variables?

ng-repeat special variables are:

$index

$first

$middle

$last

97. When to use $destroy() function of scope?

$destroy() - This function permanently detached the current scope with all of its children from the parent scope. This is required when child scopes are no longer needed. Hence, $destroy() function is called to remove these scopes from the browser's memory.

When $destroy() is called all the watchers and listeners get removed and the object which represented the scope becomes eligible for garbage collection.

98. How to detect swipe event in mobile browsers/devices in AngularJS?

The ngTouch library provides swipe directives to capture user swipes, either left or right across the screen. These events are useful when the user want to swipe to the next photo gallery photo or to a new portion of our app.

The ngSwipeLeft directive detects when an HTML element is swiped from the right to the left and the ngSwipeRight directive detects when an HTML element is swiped from the left to the right.

99. How to do animation with the help of AngularJS?

AngularJS 1.2 comes with animation support via ngAnimate module. To enable animations within your angular app, you need to link the angular-animate.js file and include ngAnimate module as a dependency within your angular app.

100. How $timeout and window.setTimeout work in AngularJS?

$timeout is an Angular service which wraps the browser's window.setTimeout() function into a try/catch block and delegates any exceptions to $exceptionHandler service. It is used to call a JavaScript function after a given time delay. The $timeout service only schedules a single call to the function.

101. How to enable caching in Angular 1.x?

Caching can be enabled by setting the config.cache value or the default cache value to TRUE or to a cache object that is created with $cacheFactory.

In case you want to cache all the responses, then you can set the default cache value to TRUE.

And, if you want to cache a specific response, then you can set the config.cache value to TRUE.

102. What is a locale ID?

A locale is a specific geographical, political, or cultural region. The most commonly used locale ID consists of two parts: language code and country code. For example, en-US, en-AU, hi-IN are all valid locale IDs that have both language codes and country codes.

103. How to handle mobile browsers/devices events in AngularJS?

Mobile browsers/devices deal with events differently than desktop browsers. The AngularJS provide ngTouch library (angular-touch.js) to detect mobile browsers/devices events.

For example, Mobile browsers detect a tap event and then wait for second event about 100 milli second if any. So, if we're double-tapping the device then after this delay the browser fires a click event.

In this way this delay can make our apps unresponsive. Hence, instead of dealing with the click event, we can detect touch event using ngTouch library. It handles touch detection for us through the ng-click directive. Hence it will take care of calling the correct click event for mobile.

104. Explain AngularJS boot process?

When the page is loaded in the browser, following things happen:

HTML document is loaded into the browser and evaluated by the browser. AngularJS JavaScript file is loaded; the angular global object is created. Next, JavaScript which registers controller functions is executed.

Next AngularJS scans through the HTML to look for AngularJS apps and views. Once view is located, it connects that view to the corresponding controller function.

Next, AngularJS executes the controller functions. It then renders the views with data from the model populated by the controller. The page gets ready.

105. Which one is fast between $digest and $apply?

$digest() is faster than $apply(), since $apply() triggers watchers on the entire scope chain i.e. on the current scope and its parents or children (if it has) while $digest()

triggers watchers on the current scope and its children(if it has).

106. List some examples of exit codes ?

Examples of exit codes are:

Unused

Uncaught Fatal Exception

Fatal Error

Non-function Internal Exception Handler

Internal Exception handler Run-Time Failure

Internal JavaScript Evaluation Failure

107. Explain what is the difference between AngularJS and backbone.js?

Angular has integrated built-in utilities, which help to validate client input before it gets processed or sent to a server;

Angular has dedicated debugging tools;

Angular checks for any changes and update the corresponding fields;

Angular has a popular plugin which includes facilities to create view animations.

Backbone allows to integrate third party libraries well;

Backbone uses observables for data binding (it observes Models);

Backbone has a possibility to be extended in order to support models and views updating each other;

Backbone might work well with other template engines

108. Why to use AngularJS?

There are following reasons to choose AngularJS as a web development framework:

It is based on MVC pattern which helps you to organize your web apps or web application properly.

It extends HTML by attaching directives to your HTML markup with new attributes or tags and expressions in order to define very powerful templates.

It also allows you to create your own directives, making reusable components that fill your needs and abstract your DOM manipulation logic.

It supports two-way data binding i.e. connects your HTML (views) to your JavaScript objects (models) seamlessly. In this way any change in model will update the view and vice versa without any DOM manipulation or event handling.

It encapsulates the behavior of your application in controllers which are instantiated with the help of dependency injection.

It supports services that can be injected into your controllers to use some utility code to fulfil your need. For example, it provides $http service to communicate with REST service.

It supports dependency injection which helps you to test your angular app code very easily.

Also, AngularJS is mature community to help you. It has widely support over the internet.

****

Please check this out: Our other best-selling books are-

500+ Java & J2EE Interview Questions & Answers-Java & J2EE Programming

200+ Frequently Asked Interview Questions & Answers in iOS Development

200 + Frequently Asked Interview Q & A in SQL , PL/SQL, Database Development &   Administration

200+ Frequently Asked Interview Questions & Answers in Manual Testing

100+ Frequently Asked Interview Questions & Answers in Scala

100+ Frequently Asked Interview Q & A in Swift Programming

100+ Frequently Asked Interview Q & A in Python Programming

100+ Frequently Asked Interview Questions & Answers in Android Development

Frequently asked Interview Q & A in Java programming

Frequently Asked Interview Questions & Answers in J2EE

Frequently asked Interview Q & A in Mobile Testing

Frequently asked Interview Q & A in Test Automation-Selenium Testing

www.ingramcontent.com/pod-product-compliance
Lightning Source LLC
LaVergne TN
LVHW041221050326
832903LV00021B/738